THE PROPHESY OF
ROBERT LOUIS STEVENSON

DAMIEN
OF MOLOKAI

THE LEPER SAINT

Washington DC 11 June 2010

Bob,

THE PROPHESY OF
ROBERT LOUIS STEVENSON

DAMIEN
OF MOLOKAI

THE LEPER SAINT

Thank you for your kindness and hospitality. I am most grateful.

Introduction by Fr F.E. Burns PE
Afterword and cover illustration by Rev. Keith Drury

Editor & Foreword: DON MULLAN

Best wishes,

a little book company

First published in 2009 by
a little book company
11 Hillsbrook Crescent
Perrystown
Dublin 12
Ireland
Tel/Fax: +353 1 455 5453
e-mail: albc@eircom.net
www: alittlebookcompany.com

ISBN 978-1-906077-05-1

Cover Image: Rev. Keith Drury
Cover Design: Glen Powell
Typesetting and Book Design: Glen Powell
Printed in Ireland by Beta Printing Services

To the memory of my friend
Jim McShane
(aka Baltimora)
1957–1995

And

To my friend
Fr Jim O'Halloran SDB
a missionary priest who
like Fr Damien of Molokai
has lived a life of faithfulness and goodness

THE SAINTS ARE THE SINNERS
WHO KEPT ON TRYING

Robert Louis Stevenson

CONTENTS

Don Mullan, Foreword:
When Damien of Molokai Shall Be Named a Saint   1

Fr F.E. Burns, Introduction:
The Father of All who Love Goodness   29

Robert Louis Stevenson:
An Open Letter to the Rev. Dr Hyde   45

Rev. Keith Drury, Afterword:
The Grace to See It   71

Rev. Keith Drury:
Artist's Statement   80

Further Reading   82

Acknowledgements   83

Desmond Tutu HIV Foundation   85

When Damien of Molokai Shall Be Named a Saint

The political and journalistic world can boast of very few heroes who compare with Father Damien of Molokai. It is worthwhile to look for the sources of such heroism.

– Mahatma Gandhi

Children need heroes. My mother understood that. She understood that strong role models can inspire and motivate children to grow into respectful and caring citizens; citizens who try to make the world around them a better place; citizens who recognise that family extends beyond the confines of one's home and includes the downtrodden and marginalised.

It was at my mother's knee that I first learned of Fr Damien, the Belgian priest who died from leprosy on the island of Molokai. It was the early 1960s in Derry, Ireland, and I was only seven or eight years old. But the stories she told me of Fr Damien left a lasting impression.

Years later, in 1979, I left my home town to visit a hospital in southern India that specialised in the care of patients with leprosy. What I witnessed there remains a source of inspiration. The hospital was run by the Franciscan Missionaries of Mary, amongst them some Irish sisters, one of whom was the wonderful Sr Eileen Naughton.

At first I found it difficult to look at the deformities caused by the disease: hands and feet that looked like mangled clumps; frightened eyes that peered from behind faces swollen with what appeared to be boiling skin and fish scales. Through the compassionate eyes of Sr Eileen I soon learned to see the human being trapped within the deformity. The human being that this gracious and gentle Irish missionary and her colleagues loved and cared for.

I travelled with Sr Eileen by bicycle to outlying villages, where she checked families for the early tell-tale signs of white blotches on their flesh. There was still a stigma attached to the disease and those infected were in danger of becoming outcasts, condemned to lives of deplorable suffering and isolation.

Back at the hospital in Fatimanagar in the state of Tamil Nadu, I discovered that the preferred name for the illness was not leprosy but Hansen's disease. The deliberate use of this name was just one aspect of the hospital's work to eradicate the ancient prejudices associated with the condition. Prejudices that claimed the sufferer was either cursed or being punished for a personal or family sin.

Mercifully, in 1873, the same year that Fr Damien volunteered to minister to the lepers of Molokai, Dr G. H. Armauer Hansen of Norway had discovered that the source of the malady was a germ, *Mycobacterium leprae*. It took, however, another seventy years to find a cure.

At the Franciscan Missionaries of Mary Hospital I found the same heroic compassion that Fr Damien brought to Molokai; though the carers, by then, had the benefit of scientific and medical discoveries, the absence of which set the young Belgian priest on the road to selfless martyrdom.

Miracles were performed daily at the hospital. To this day I retain a small oil painting, gifted to me by a former sufferer of the disease who had been cured at the hospital and who worked there with his wife, also a sufferer. The painting depicts a deer standing by a river in a mountainous valley. At the bottom, in Tamil, he wrote the words of Psalm 23: 'Near restful waters he leads me, to revive my drooping spirit.'

For the outcasts of Molokai, Fr Damien's arrival and ministry helped to revive many broken spirits as he set about creating a community that made them feel, once again, human. He did not bring a cure to Molokai but he brought something far more powerful and compelling: a human ministry that was pregnant with the love and compassion of God.

Fr Damien

Damien was born Jozef de Veuster on 3 January 1840 in Tremelo, Belgium, the seventh child of Flemish parents, Frans de Veuster and Cato Wouters. Frans was a corn merchant and sent Jozef to college at Braine-le-Comte to prepare for a career in commerce. However, in 1858, following a retreat given by Redemptorist missionaries, the teenager made the decision to become a priest.

Jozef entered the noviciate of the Congregation of the Sacred Hearts of Jesus and Mary in Leuven, near Brussels, in 1859. His decision to join the Congregation, also known as the Picpus Fathers, was influenced by his older brother Auguste, who was already a member and who had taken the religious name of Fr Pamphile.

Jozef made his first vows on 7 October 1860, taking the religious name of Damien, presumed to be after St Damian, the twin brother of St Cosmas. Saints Damian and Cosmas were healers in the seaport of Aegea (modern Ayas) in the Gulf of Issus. They suffered martyrdom, along with three younger brothers, around 287 AD.

Fr Pamphile had aspired to serve in the Congregation's mission on the Pacific islands of the Kingdom of Hawaii. When poor health prevented him from travelling, his younger brother volunteered to take his place. Damien stepped ashore at Honolulu Harbour on 19 March 1864. Two months later, on 21 May, he was ordained to the priesthood at the Cathedral of Our Lady of Peace, Honolulu, and assigned to North Kohala.

European and American missionaries often brought their own cultural prejudices and ignorance to the territories they wished to Christianise. In their urgent quest to save souls, they had little tolerance of the unique heritage of other cultures. The Pacific islanders' rich heritage of ancient chants, songs and dances that told mythical stories of love and the power of nature in a paradise that emerged from fire and lava was frowned upon as an inferior culture that must be changed. Conversion, therefore, involved more than a new religion, it required the adoption of Western values and attitudes.

As a young missionary Damien was not immune to such prejudices. He wrote to his parents:

> Here I am a priest, dear parents, here I am a missionary in a corrupt, heretical, idolatrous country. How great my obligations are! Ah! Do not forget this poor priest running night and day over the volcanoes night and day in search of strayed sheep. Pray night and day for me, I beg you.

Damien's time in Hawaii coincided with a public health crisis, which saw the native islanders dying in their thousands from diseases introduced by foreign traders and sailors. These diseases included influenza, syphilis and the dreaded affliction of leprosy.

Molokai

The deformities associated with leprosy resulted in the widespread shunning of its victims. Fuelled by ignorance, fear of contamination gripped the populace. In an effort to check the spread of the illness, the King of Hawaii, Kamehameha V, decided to quarantine the lepers in an isolated colony at Kalaupapa, Kalawao County, on the north side of the island of Molokai.

Access to the Kalaupapa peninsula was restricted by a steep mountain ridge and great cliffs that stood defiant against the power of the Pacific Ocean. The Hawaiian administration saw the colony's physical geography as a symbolic buffer between its people and the encroachment of the disease. For the suffering exiles, however, the setting deepened the sense of isolation, abandonment and condemnation that they suddenly had to endure.

The Hawaiian Royal Board of Health, with responsibility for the colony, failed to provide sufficient medical support and resources and gradually the colony descended into a living hell. Visitors to Molokai brought back horror stories that gripped the entire kingdom with fear and trepidation.

The head of the Catholic Mission to Hawaii, Monsignor Louis Désiré Maigret, a member of the Picpus

Fathers, believed the lepers should be afforded a priest to minister to their spiritual needs. As close contact with lepers carried a high risk of contamination and might ultimately condemn the person to death, Monsignor Maigret decided to seek volunteers amongst his order to go to Molokai for short periods of service on a rota system.

Damien volunteered. He arrived at the Kalaupapa colony on 10 May 1873 with Monsignor Maigret, who introduced him to the 816 lepers living there. Once settled, Damien quickly realised that this community of abandoned humanity would need long-term spiritual care and the tools, literally, to build a new society. He made it clear that he was there for the long haul.

Having set aside any fear of contagion, Damien's ministry embraced the lepers of Molokai both spiritually and physically. He greeted them as his brothers and sisters, fearlessly cleaning sores and open wounds and dressing ulcers caused by the disease. One of his first acts of mercy was to clean the side of a young girl whose infected wounds were wreathing with worms.

Symbolically these acts were very important. By the simple act of touching his leper community, Damien transmitted the power of God's transforming love. As well as bandaging their wounds, Damien anointed the sick with holy oil, placed Holy Communion in their mouths, dined with them and sometimes helped to clean the houses of his bedridden parishioners.

Damien was not immune to the horrors that surrounded him. In his earliest writings he vividly described his sense of revulsion at the obnoxious odour the disease released and explained how he tried to cope:

> Many a time in fulfilling my priestly duties at the lepers' homes, I have been obliged, not only to close my nostrils, but to remain outside to breathe fresh air. To counteract the bad smell, I got myself accustomed to the use of tobacco. The smell of the pipe preserved me somewhat from carrying in my clothes the obnoxious odour of our lepers.

We Lepers

Damien identified with the lepers. It is often told that after he contracted leprosy he stood before his congregation and addressed them as 'we lepers'. However, the truth is that Damien had always used the word 'we' in his sermons on Molokai. During his first year there he wrote to his brother, Fr Pamphile, in Belgium, 'I make myself a leper with the lepers to gain all to Jesus Christ. That is why, in preaching, I say "we lepers": not, "my brethren" ...'

One of the most moving and compassionate of Damien's achievements on Molokai was demonstrating the value of each leper's life through the dignity he afforded them upon death. The cemetery, located close to his chapel, was a virtual dumping ground where shallow graves were ravaged at night by scavenging animals and rodents. To protect the graves, he had the cemetery fenced off. He then arranged for the construction of coffins and for the digging of deeper graves upon which the names of the deceased were recorded. He established a Christian Burial Association, which organised requiem Masses for the deceased with proper funeral rites and the playing of sacred music during funeral processions.

In addition to ministering to the sacramental needs of the colony, Damien launched himself into a major social project that transformed the Molokai mission. He recognised that his forsaken community had brought with them the same talents and skills they had possessed on their Pacific island homelands. Amongst them were carpenters, builders, labourers, farmers, teachers, artists and musicians. Therein lay the very foundations and fabric of a new society. A structured society capable of developing with dignity, irrespective of the deformities leprosy wrought upon its members' human frames.

There was no time for self-pity. There was much to be done and Damien needed all the help he could get as he sought to establish the Parish of St Philomena. He organised crews who took responsibility for constructing the buildings that the community needed: workshops, orphanages, schools, farms, a hospital, new houses, a rectory, a church, even an excellent road between the island villages of Kalawao and Kalaupapa.

Damien also encouraged the creation of choirs and marching bands, for which he obtained instruments. He experienced great joy in watching these groups perform traditional and sacred music at community celebrations, concerts and religious ceremonies.

Damien's love was infectious and it did not take long for the people to respond to his exhortations to live lives of human dignity and respect. Many of their once drab and dilapidated shacks, dwellings that had oozed depression and hopelessness, soon became brightly painted homes with newly planted vegetable gardens.

News of Damien's work began to spread and the Hawaiian people, both on and off the island of Molokai, were deeply moved by his selfless humanity. They reciprocated with their own love and trust in his mission.

In 1888, Englishman Edward Clifford visited Molokai. He later wrote:

> I had gone to Molokai expecting to find it scarcely less dreadful than hell itself ... the cheerful people, the lovely landscapes, and comparatively painless life were all surprises. These poor people seemed singularly happy.

Clifford questioned lepers about their existence on Molokai and whether they missed the island homelands from which they had been removed. He recorded the following reply:

> Oh, no! We're well off here. The government watches over us, the superintendent is good, and we like our pastor. He builds our houses himself, he gives us tea,

biscuits, sugar and clothes. He takes good care of us and doesn't let us want for anything.

Human Frailty

What I find most appealing about Damien is his human frailty. There is no evidence of a man who cured the sick or gave sight to the blind – powers one might expect such a holy soul to possess. And not everyone loved him. Some government officials in Honolulu considered him headstrong and obstinate and were quick to complain to the Bishop of Honolulu about his ceaseless demands on behalf of the lepers of Molokai.

Even amongst his confrères there was resentment, even jealousy. As his notoriety increased beyond the islands of Hawaii, the Superiors of his Congregation were concerned that it might appear that Damien was the only missionary willing to serve on the colony. This, of course, was not true. The Congregation sent three assistants to support his work but they did not bond. Consequently, he was accused of being a loner.

Damien's sense of loneliness and isolation was, at times, oppressive and depressing. He wrote of feelings of melancholy and of 'black thoughts' from not having a religious companion with whom he could confess and enjoy the benefits of the sacraments. Despite this, he strove to live a life entirely faithful to his religious vows. After his death one of his notebooks was found to contain the following revelation:

> Be severe toward yourself, indulgent toward others. Have scrupulous exactitude for everything regarding God: prayer, meditation, Mass, administration of the Sacraments. Unite your heart with God … Remember always your three vows, by which you are dead to the things of the world. Remember always that God is eternal and work courageously in order one day to be united with him forever.

On one occasion, Damien was prevented from boarding a ship in order to confess his sins to the bishop travelling on board. The ship's captain could not be persuaded to overlook the government's isolation policy and so Damien asked the bishop to hear his confession at a distance. The bishop agreed, and Damien made a touching public confession across the waves.

Fr Damien's Leprosy

Damien spent many hours each day walking the length and breadth of the colony and developed a nightly ritual of soothing his feet by bathing them in hot water. In December 1884 he had noted that his feet had lost the sensation of heat. It was the first indication that he had succumbed to Hansen's disease. His response to this death sentence was to work even harder to alleviate the suffering of his parishioners.

With the onset of the disease Damien's sense of urgency increased. Of paramount importance was the need to ensure that the work he had started would live beyond his death. With a grateful heart he began to welcome important volunteers who came to Molokai to support him. Each brought essential skills that allowed Damien to find consolation in the knowledge that the decade of devotion he had expended, would continue.

Fr Louis Lambert Conrardy, a fellow Belgian working in the United States, was granted permission by the Archbishop of Oregon, Dr William Gross, to join Damien in Molokai to assist his pastoral ministry. Archbishop Gross wrote:

> I have trampled all over Oregon with Fr. Conrardy
> and he is a noble, heroic man ... Though he knows
> and realises perfectly that he might succumb to the
> disease, his voluntary going is real heroism.

Fr Conrardy proved to be the spiritual companion that
Damien had longed for, supporting and encouraging him
in his extraordinary pastoral mission until the end.

At Damien's request Mother Marianne Cope, Superior
of the Franciscan Sisters of Syracuse, arrived with three
sisters who set up a small hospital and helped care for the
girls' orphanage on Molokai.

Joseph Dutton, an American Civil War veteran and
recovering alcoholic, took over the duties of construction
and maintenance of buildings and served in the boys'
home. He arrived in July 1886 and remained on Molokai
until his death in 1931, aged eighty.

James Sinnett, a nurse from Chicago, assisted Mother
Marianne and nursed Fr Damien through the last phases
of his illness. Sinnett, whom Damien affectionately called
'Brother James', served also as the Belgian missionary's
secretary in his final months. It was James Sinnett who
closed Damien's eyes after he had expired. Shortly after

Damien's death, Sinnett left Molokai, never to be heard of again.

Damien's love and respect for his parishioners attracted the prejudices of Christian fundamentalists who believed leprosy was the inevitable result of lives of idolatry and immorality. Indeed there were some, including doctors, who believed that leprosy could only be spread through sexual contact. Such people suggested that Damien's own leprosy was the result of immoral living.

Damien was acutely aware of these painful accusations and had no hesitation in humbly presenting himself for a full medical examination before Dr Arning, a world-renowned specialist in the disease. Dr Arning reported that Damien had no sign of any sexually transmitted diseases. And shortly before he died, Damien dictated a statement to Joseph Dutton, in which he declared, 'I have never had sexual intercourse with anyone whomsoever.'

The Death of Fr Damien
Fr Damien died of leprosy on 15 April 1889, aged forty-nine. He was buried alongside the other lepers near St Philomena's Church. Within a year, a global discussion

was under way on the merits of Damien's missionary work. This sometimes bitter debate is, in part, the inspiration for this book, 120 years later.

Meanwhile on Molokai, Mother Marianne continued in Damien's footsteps and helped realise much of his vision for the community. She remained there until her death of natural causes in 1918. The work of Mother Marianne and her sisters on Molokai, while somewhat eclipsed by Damien, deserves special recognition.

In 1941, a reporter from Utica, New York – where Marianne had helped to establish one of the first registered hospitals in the United States – interviewed a nurse who had cared for Marianne in her final years. The nurse recalled her as 'the gentlest, cheeriest and most dignified person you could imagine, and a disciplinarian, too'.

Of particular importance was the insight the nurse gave to the work that Marianne continued after the death of Damien:

> She revolutionized life on Molokai, brought cleanliness, pride and fun to the colony. People on Molokai laugh now – like other people in the world, laugh at the same things, the same dilemmas and jokes.

It was Mother Marianne who bought the girls hair ribbons and pretty things to wear, dresses and scarves. Women keep their cottages and their rooms in the big communal houses neatly, pridefully. There are snowy bedspreads, pictures on the walls. They set their tables at meal time with taste, Mother Marianne brought that about.

She interested the women in color harmony. Sit in services at the back of the church in Molokai and observe the lovely arrangements of color of the women. When Mother Marianne went to the island, people there had no thought for the graces of life. 'We are lepers,' they told her. 'What does it matter?' Well, she changed all that. Doctors have said that her psychology was 50 years ahead of her time.

The population of the Molokai leper colony peaked at 1,174 in 1890 and by the time the isolation law was eventually repealed in 1969 over eight thousand people had been forcibly exiled there. The area was designated a national historical park in 1980 and the few remaining survivors finally received an official apology in 2008.

At the request of the Belgian government, Damien's remains were returned to his native land in 1936 and interred in the crypt of the Church of the Congregation of the Sacred Hearts at Leuven, not far from the village of his birth. Following his beatification in 1995, a relic of Damien's body was returned to Hawaii.

Inspiration and Canonisation

The title of this book takes its inspiration from the letter penned by the celebrated Scottish writer, Robert Louis Stevenson, a devout Presbyterian, who prophesied that Fr Damien would, one day, be declared a Saint of the Roman Catholic Church. Catholic devotion to Damien began shortly after his death with people around the world seeking his intercession.

Reports of Damien's intervention in the lives of the faithful were rigorously investigated by the Vatican during the twentieth century. On 7 July 1977 Pope Paul VI declared Damien 'Venerable'. For the purpose of beatification and canonisation miracles are required. The first miracle attributed to Damien's intercession is said to have occurred on 11 September 1895, after a French nun, Sr Simplicia Hue, began a nine-day novena to Fr

Damien, less than seven years after his death. Sr Hue was dying of an intestinal disease but it disappeared after she began the novena. She lived for another thirty-two years. This first miracle led to Damien's beatification on 4 June 1995, in Belgium, by Pope John Paul II.

On 11 October 2009, Blessed Damien was canonised by Pope Benedict XVI at St Peter's Basilica in Rome. This followed Pope Benedict XVI's approval, in 2008, of a second miracle attributed to Damien's intercession. Audrey Toguchi, from Honolulu, was declared to have recovered from an incurable form of cancer after she prayed at Damien's grave in Kalaupapa during two visits to Molokai in late 1998. Doctors who treated Toguchi said a malignant tumour continued to decrease and the cancer eventually disappeared.

Damien's work has not been forgotten by the wider population either. He has been the subject of various works of art and literature, television documentaries, and cinema and theatre productions. A bronze statue of Damien stands both at Statuary Hall at the United States Capitol and in front of the Hawaii State Capitol.

Damien continues to touch the lives of many people, from schoolchildren to world figures. Mahatma Gandhi is one of many humanitarian leaders to have been influenced by Damien's selfless commitment to the lepers of Molokai. Schools, community groups and non-profit organisations around the world have adopted his name. In Ireland, for example, 'Damien House', located near Cootehill, Co. Cavan, takes inspiration from the Belgian missionary who 'brought hope where there was despair and acceptance where there was rejection'.

In 2005 Father Damien was given the title 'De Grootste Belg' – the Greatest Belgian – following a poll conducted by the Flemish Radio and Television Network, Vlaamse Radio- en Televisieomroep (VRT).

Damien had found a colony of rejected, neglected and desperate people when he arrived on the Kalaupapa peninsula. He offered them respect, acceptance and love. He worked tirelessly on their behalf and when he died, sixteen years later, he left behind a stronger, more caring community of people who had rediscovered their human dignity. His life and dedication are an example for all.

Fittingly, Damien has become the unofficial patron of those with HIV and AIDS – another stigmatised community who suffer from the same ignorance and prejudice as the lepers of Molokai.

Bishop Patrick K. Lynch, Auxiliary Bishop to Southwark, England, and a member of Fr Damien's congregation, has written the following reflection for the congregation's Irish website:

> Today as then, the world knows rejected persons of all kinds: the incurably ill (victims of AIDS or other diseases), abandoned children, disoriented youths, exploited women, neglected elderly people, oppressed minorities. For all who suffer, Damien remains the voice reminding us that the infinite love of God is full of compassion and consolation, confidence and hope, his is a voice that denounces injustice. In Damien we can all recognize the herald of the Good News. Like the Good Samaritan, he went to the aid of those whom sickness had cast aside along the road. This is what makes Damien an example for all men and women who wish to be involved in the struggle for a more just, more humane world, a society more conformed to the heart of God.
>
> Damien is and remains for all the servant of the human person, the servant of a humanity that needs to live, but even more needs reasons for living.
>
> This is the Damien who challenges us even today!

Damien continues to be an inspirational role model. His universal appeal is what has inspired this book. The Roman Catholic priesthood has suffered gravely in recent years from the shocking revelations that some priests abused positions of sacred trust in their dealings with young people. Yet it is important that we remember there have also been many priests who have struggled to live authentic lives of heroic selflessness in humble imitation of the carpenter of Nazareth. I have had the privilege, in Ireland, Brazil, and throughout the world, to meet many.

Despite the often scandalous, acrimonious and embarrassing disputes that divide Christian denominations and world religions that profess their belief in a God of Love and compassion, symbols of unity arise in which we recognise the personification of core spiritual and gospel values; values that manifest themselves in an all-embracing goodness. Mahatma Gandhi, His Holiness the Dalai Lama, the Rev. Martin Luther King Jr, Archbishop Desmond Tutu and Mother Teresa of Calcutta are examples that spring to mind. Fr Damien de Veuster was also a magnet of mercy and goodness who gathered a wide diversity of friends from across the globe; friends who represented different faiths and philosophies but who found in Damien a source of light and love.

The robust defence of Damien penned by Robert Louis Stevenson in the face of what the celebrated Scottish writer saw as an unjust attack by a fellow Presbyterian is, at once, a wonderful ecumenical gesture towards a Roman Catholic priest, and another example of how Damien's ministry inspired people of all faiths and none.

Reflecting on this aspect of Damien's life, Bishop Patrick K. Lynch writes:

Damien was before all else a Catholic missionary and also a man of his time. While he remains convinced in his own belief, he respects the religious convictions of others, he accepts them as persons and receives with joy their collaboration and their help. With a heart wide open to the most abject and miserable, he shows no difference in his approach and in his care of the 'lepers'. Whether in his parish ministry or his works of charity he finds a place for everyone. Among his best friends is the Lutheran Meyer, superintendent of the 'leper colony', the Anglican Clifford, the painter, the free-thinker Moritz, the doctor on Molokai, the Buddhist Goto, the Japanese leprologist.

Damien is very far from being just a philanthropist or a hero for the day! People from all creeds and from all philosophical systems recognize in him the servant of God which he always reveals himself to be, and they respect his passion for the salvation of souls.

Servant of Humanity

I hope that this book is yet another example of Damien's ability to bring diverse people together. The book is dedicated to two friends: one, a childhood friend, Jim McShane from Derry who died of AIDS in 1995 at a time when prejudice and ignorance added to the intensity of his isolation and suffering; and to Fr Jim O'Halloran, a friend since 1979, who, like Damien, devoted his priestly ministry to the downtrodden and marginalised across a lifetime of faithfulness and great goodness. Apart from the centrepiece of the book, Robert Louis Stevenson's letter, my three collaborators in creating this book have been a Roman Catholic priest from Australia, Fr F.E. Burns; a Presbyterian minister and artist from Belfast, Rev. Keith Drury; and Archbishop Desmond Tutu, Anglican Archbishop Emeritus of Southern Africa, whose HIV Foundation will receive royalties from this publication.

Details of the Foundation are given at the end of the book and readers are encouraged to support this important mission. Given the support that Damien's own mission received from members of the Anglican Communion, I have no doubt that he would warmly approve.

When declaring Fr Damien 'Blessed' on Pentecost Sunday 1995, Pope John Paul II also gave him the title 'Servant of Humanity'. This book is published to commemorate the day of Damien's canonisation, 11 October 2009, and was inspired by another great lover of humanity, Robert Louis Stevenson, who, in his famous letter of 25 February 1890, prophesised this very day:

'when Damien of Molokai shall be named a Saint'

Don Mullan
Dublin, Ireland
11 October 2009

INTRODUCTION

The Father of All who Love Goodness

> Damien ... is my father ... and the father of all who
> love goodness.
> – Robert Louis Stevenson

The editor of the *Sydney Morning Herald* was delighted
to receive a bulky, hand-delivered envelope on 25
February 1890, which clearly showed the sender's details
as Robert Louis Stevenson, c/- The Union Club, Bligh
Street, Sydney. On previous visits to Sydney the famous
author had been the toast of the town, meeting with local
literary and artistic figures, among them J.F. Archibald,
Arthur Streeton and Tom Roberts. The now chronically
ill Stevenson remained much in demand and had given a

number of interviews during his present visit, some of them from his sickbed. When the editor read the letter Stevenson had submitted for publication, however, the blood slowly drained from his face.

The long letter was an outspoken and powerful defence of Fr Damien de Veuster, the leper priest who had died the previous April and who had been the subject of a bitter sectarian attack. Stevenson's response was written 'both in anger and in haste' and the *Herald's* legal advice was strongly against its publication. It would be difficult to exaggerate the significance of these events.

In writing the letter, Stevenson did a great deal more than defend one individual: in the face of enormous opposition he spoke out against evil and injustice on behalf of 'all who love goodness'. Sectarianism was rife in the 1890s, yet here was a well-established, world-famous Protestant figure defending a Catholic priest. In doing so he risked (and subsequently incurred) the ire of the Establishment and many others, including some of his own denomination. As a lawyer, he knew that his letter was libellous and declared that he fully expected to be sued. Whatever people may have thought of his judgment, they could not doubt the force of his convictions.

As a boy I had read the almost unbelievable story of Fr Damien and it was used in school as a modern example that Christ can be found among the least of his brothers and sisters. I had also read Stevenson's fictional works, including *The Strange Case of Dr Jekyll and Mr Hyde* and *Treasure Island*. It was much later that I came across 'An Open Letter to the Rev. Dr Hyde', but I found this classic piece of invective quite overpowering. I still do. No wonder the *Sydney Morning Herald* would not touch it!

In Stevenson's native Scotland things were different, however, and the letter was soon published in Edinburgh. Robert Louis' words then thundered across the literary world. Although the Open Letter was widely published, Stevenson refused to accept any payment or reward, not even 'a penny bread roll'. All royalties went to the Damien Institute at Molokai.

Stevenson's outrage had been sparked by the events following Fr Damien's death. Damien's courageous life had been widely celebrated, even in the secular press, prompting the Rev. H.B. Gage, a Californian minister, to write to Rev. Dr C.M. Hyde of Honolulu for further details of the suddenly famous priest. Hyde replied that Damien was 'no saintly philanthropist', rather he was 'a coarse, dirty, headstrong bigot ... not a pure man in his relations with women', and claimed that his leprosy was 'due to his vices and carelessness'. In an example of bigotry at its mischief-making worst, Gage proceeded to have Hyde's description of Damien published in the United States and as far afield as the *Sydney Presbyterian*, where, unfortunately for both Gage and Hyde, it was read by Stevenson.

At first Stevenson could not believe what he was reading. He knew Hyde and had been his guest when he lived in Honolulu. He had also, against his own doctor's advice – Stevenson had TB, visited Molokai shortly after Damien's death. He had been impressed by the many stories he had heard and was keen to learn more, though he admitted to being 'cynical about popular heroes'.

Stevenson's visit to Molokai lasted eight days, but his awakening began even before he landed there. He travelled in a small boat with two nuns, as he relates, 'bidding farewell (in humble imitation of Damien) to the lights and joys of life'. One of the nuns 'wept silently and I could not withhold myself from joining her ... as the boat drew nearer we ... beheld the stairs crowded with abominable deformations of our common manhood ... a population as

A short letter written by Fr Damien, circa early 1889, asking Dr Swift to visit him on Molokai
Source: Talbot Collection, Georgetown University Library

Above and below, two iconic portraits of Fr Damien de Veuster, as a young missionary and shortly before his death
Source: SSCC Congregazione dei Sacri Cuori di Gesu e di Maria

Fr Damien with members of his children's choir
Source: SSCC Congregazione dei Sacri Cuori di Gesu e di Maria

A portrait of Robert Louis Stevenson with the celebrated American writer Mark Twain, by Francis Luis Mora, 1907
Source: Grill Collection of the National Arts Club

The tomb of Fr Damien, St Anthony's Chapel, Leuven, Belgium
Source: Don Mullan (Nokia N95)

St Anthony's Chapel, Leuven, Belgium
Source: Don Mullan (Nokia N95)

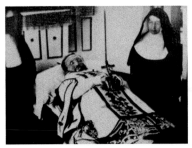

Fr Damien, at peace
Source: SSCC Congregazione dei Sacri Cuori
di Gesu e di Maria

The community of Molokai remember their
beloved pastor
Source: SSCC Congregazione dei Sacri Cuori
di Gesu e di Maria

Mother Marianne Cope, who
continued the work of
Fr Damien and died on
Molokai in 1918
Source: SSCC Congregazione dei Sacri
Cuori di Gesu e di Maria

Stained glass window depicting Fr Damien's mission on
Molokai, St Anthony's Chapel, Leuven
Source: Don Mullan (Nokia N95)

Fr Damien's burial place until the return of his remains to Belgium in 1936
Source: Fathers Patrick and Brian Corcoran

St Philomena's Church, Molokai, undergoing renovations in advance of Fr Damien's canonisation.
In the distance can be seen Damien's grave. In the foreground the burial place of Joseph Dutton,
who joined Damien in 1886 and never left the island. He died in 1931.
Source: Fathers Patrick and Brian Corcoran

Audrey Toguchi, whose recovery from an incurable form of cancer in 1999 was the second miracle attributed to the intercession of Fr Damien
Source: Hugh E. Gentry/AP

1979, Fatimanagar, Tamil Nadu, India. Editor, Don Mullan, visiting a family in an outlying village who were being monitored and treated for the early signs of Hansen's disease.
Source: Sr Eileen Naughton

Damien's compassion depicted in this statue at St Anthony's Chapel, Leuven, Belgium
Source: Don Mullan (Nokia N95)

Limited edition of 100 prints available. Each personally signed and numbered by the artist.
Size (A2) 420 x 594mm.

50% of all procceds will be donated to The Desmond Tutu HIV Foundation. (Rev K. Drury's work
and ministry is fully supported by his career as an artist allowing him to engage with a variety of
different projects, locally or internationally.)

Price:
Framed £245
Unframed £195 (inc p+p)
For postal reasons it is best to ship unframed.

Purchase online or contact the artist directly
www.artobiography.co.uk
keith@artobiography.co.uk
Mobile +44 (0) 78 6633 9920
Tel +44 (0) 28 91811191

only now and then surrounds us in the horror of a nightmare … the butt-ends of human beings lying there almost unrecognisable, but still breathing, still thinking, still remembering … a pitiful place to visit, a hell to dwell in'.

But dwell in it he did. Stevenson became very friendly with the nuns and, to their despair, mixed freely with the lepers and played with the children. His sorry state of health increased his chances of infection and Sr Marianne admonished him.

Stevenson was a deeply spiritual man, honest to the point of bluntness, and above all a truth-seeker. What he saw in Molokai simply overwhelmed him. As a younger man he had often joked about the clergy of his own denomination in Edinburgh, saying that if they had appeared more as joyful bearers of the Word, and less like undertakers, he may have taken more notice. Fr Damien's hands-on approach to Christianity, together with his robust faith and his acceptance of the news of his own leprosy 'with a merry heart', was something different. Stevenson was well aware of Damien's human failings, noting that 'he was no plaster saint', but the evidence of his goodness was undeniable.

Stevenson, who belonged to the celebrated Scottish family of 'Lighthouse' Stevenson – famous in his own right as a man of letters and a student of both law and engineering, declared that the eight days on Fr Damien's Molokai changed his life.

Before leaving the island, Stevenson presented the children's home with many gifts and promised them a piano 'so there will always be music'. The piano was later shipped from Honolulu. To the nuns, he dedicated the following poem:

To the Reverend Sister Marianne,
Matron of the Bishop Home, Kalaupapa.

To see the infinite pity of this place,
The mangled limb, the devastated face,
The innocent sufferers smiling at the rod,
A fool were tempted to deny his God.

He sees, and shrinks; but if he looks again,
Lo, beauty springing from the breasts of pain,
He marks the sisters on the painful shores,
And even a fool is silent and adores.

Just as a cursory reading of Stevenson's Open Letter gives evidence of his strength of character, the details of his days on Molokai reveal a special gentleness. Mother Marianne Cope recorded her impressions of his humanity 'as we looked over the place together': he was 'sensitive ... quick to love ... he sought out the cases most in need of sympathy ... [those] beyond all hope of relief. He seemed more and more moved with compassion.' He taught the leper girls to play croquet, taking part in their games, 'his manner so simple and unaffected ... the girls thought he was the best white man they had ever met'.

Clearly Marianne was deeply impressed with Stevenson and, interestingly, her poignant words reveal that she was unaware of his celebrity at the time of his visit. Perhaps she never learnt that her admiration for Robert Louis was matched by that of her famous countryman Mark Twain, who frequently referred to his Scottish friend with affection. Marianne concludes, 'I never saw him again. Later when I knew who my visitor was, and that he had settled nearby, his visit came back to me with fresh force ... And I was glad, when I looked at our craggy sea-walled cliffs, that this gentle writer had found his resting place on the beautiful island of Samoa.'

When Stevenson read Hyde's letter, he reacted immediately: his wife reported that he locked himself in his room, muttering as he wrote his response. Stevenson believed Fr Damien to be a saint, and predicted that the Church would one day canonise him. He also believed that Hyde's contribution would be used by the Devil's Advocate as evidence against Damien's canonisation and therefore needed to be balanced by the truth, which indeed it was. I wonder if Hyde ever reflected on the irony of it all: his poisonous response to Gage was the catalyst that produced the sort of publicity (for Damien) that advertising agents dream about. Coupled with the noble honesty of wordsmith Stevenson, knowledge of Damien's dedicated goodness reached a wider audience.

The public reaction was predictable and powerful. Hyde, perhaps daunted by the way things had developed, decided not to sue, and tried to dismiss Stevenson as 'a bohemian crank, a negligible person whose opinion is of no value to anyone'. He had been particularly stung by Stevenson's closing words to him: 'The man who did what Damien did is my father ... and the father of all who love goodness ... and he was your father too, if God had given you the Grace to see it.'

It is a curious irony that the person whose reputation suffered most was not Fr Damien, who had originally been maligned; not Stevenson, though some thought he would pay for his outspokenness; not even Gage, who really betrayed Hyde; but Hyde himself. Charles McEwen Hyde was a complex character and we cannot be sure why he wrote such a harsh and damaging letter about Fr Damien. The two men had met in 1885 and shortly afterwards Hyde wrote in generous terms in the *Hawaiian Gazette* about Damien and his work. Perhaps Hyde felt that the publicity and extravagant praise for Damien following his death left the work of Hyde's church unrecognised. We can only speculate. It is important to note, however, that Hyde's letter was a personal response to Gage's request, and that it was Gage who opted to publish the letter widely, without reference to Hyde. If Gage had not acted as he did, Hyde's very human failing would never have been revealed.

A shocked Hyde had to live with the consequences, and while he did not formally apologise, he did show real remorse. In 1895 he helped establish and fund the Henry P. Baldwyn Boys' Home on Molokai, which was managed by Brother Dutton, Fr Damien's closest friend, with the members of Damien's Order. When the home was dedicated, Hyde attended and was received courteously by the Sisters of St Francis, though he noted that they might have good reason not to like him!

On his death, Damien was laid to rest by his leper friends on Molokai. Forty-six years later his remains were transferred to his native Belgium. President Franklin D. Roosevelt provided the United States Navy ship *Republic* to transport the casket to the Panama Canal. From there it was transferred to the Belgian ship *Mercator* which carried Damien to Antwerp where his remains were welcomed by the Cardinal Archbishop, King Leopold III and a crowd of more than 100,000 people.

Stevenson died just a few years later in Samoa, having made a significant mark there. He bravely and effectively helped unite and represent the Samoans – underdogs, just as Damien's lepers were – in their struggle against colonial exploitation. And when he died, aged forty-four, his native friends buried their beloved 'Great Story Teller' on the peak of Mount Vaea, 'under a wide and starry sky', as he had requested.

Speculation as to whether Stevenson later came to regret writing his famous Open Letter was, considering its enormous impact, probably inevitable. But the issue was finally settled in 1898. A former British Consul to Samoa, Sir Thomas Berry-Smith, published his essays, *Reminiscences of Stevenson*, in which he asserted that Stevenson regretted his defence of Damien 'more than anything he had ever written' and stated that, had he lived, he 'would publicly have recalled that pamphlet'. This claim brought a forceful response from the Rev. W.E. Clarke, whom Berry-Smith had quoted as his source. Clarke was a close friend of the Stevensons, he had prayed as the writer lay dying and later presided at his burial. He wrote to the editor of the *British Weekly*, denying that he had ever made such statements to Berry-Smith and declaring them to be a 'grotesque reversal of the facts'. Clarke explained that the only regret Stevenson had was giving worldwide publicity to a scandal that otherwise might have been contained 'in a very narrow circle' and scoffed at the suggestion that the publication may have been recalled, describing it as 'nonsense'.

Stevenson's widow was even more outspoken. Seeking the help of family friend Charles Stottard, Fanny wrote, 'A man named Smith, a former Consul to Samoa, has published a most malicious attack on Louis' memory. Every statement made by Sir Berry-Smith is false and has been proved so by responsible persons. The clipping I enclose to you, I wish to have copied in all the best Catholic journals. Will you do this for me? Please spread abroad the denial of the Protestant missionary the Rev. W.E. Clarke, but particularly among the Catholics. I know you will do what I ask for Louis' sake, if not for mine.'

In many ways Fr Damien de Veuster and Robert Louis Stevenson were poles apart, yet they also had much in common. They shared a fiercely dedicated love of justice and truth, and a relentless, albeit fallible, pursuit of what each saw to be right. We can safely presume that Damien would have found a conventional priestly life more comfortable, and that Stevenson may have preferred not to feel compelled to respond so powerfully to Hyde. Both men, nobly, chose the more challenging path.

Stevenson appears to have been one of those likeably uncomplicated people who accept persons and situations as they find them. His initial meeting with Hyde in Honolulu had been very cordial, his visit to Molokai had been motivated by genuine humanitarian interest, and his later reaction to what he saw as a huge injustice was swift and passionate. Despite his conflict with Hyde, Stevenson remained a loyal Presbyterian and in a sectarian age was always friendly with Catholics, who later were welcomed in their numbers by his family to gather for prayer at his deathbed.

Prayer had always been a part of daily life at Vailima, the Stevenson residence in Samoa. Robert Louis, his wife Fanny and step-son Lloyd Osbourne joined with their household of Samoan helpers each evening. Beginning with a Scripture reading, Stevenson would then pray aloud, either spontaneously or using one of the many prayers he had written, varying them to suit the occasion. They would conclude with the Our Father, and a hymn. These prayers were beautifully simple, filled with gratitude and hope, a spirit of readiness to identify with Christ in the acceptance of hardship and sorrow, and a strong belief in the Resurrection. Presbyterians, Catholics, Anglicans and Methodists all participated, reflecting a certain uncluttered ecumenism in Stevenson's character.

Not so Fr Damien, at least not at first. In his early days on Molokai he seems to have concentrated his efforts on helping only the Catholic lepers, though over the years he did soften in his attitude to others. As time passed, he treated all with equal care. Just as the disease did not discriminate, neither did he.

It is doubtful that the word 'ecumenism' was in common usage in the late nineteenth century, and ecumenism itself was practically non-existent, which makes the events that occurred in London within months of Damien's death all the more remarkable. The Rev. Hugh Chapman, an Anglican cleric, used *The Times* to publicise Damien's work and raise funds for the leper colony. Soon after, the Prince of Wales, the future King Edward VII, initiated the Fr Damien Memorial Fund. He presided at a dinner in the Hotel Metropole which was attended by, among others, the Anglican Archbishop, the Duke of Norfolk and the Duke of Fyfe. Prince Edward spoke in glowing terms of Damien's work, and announced that to date (17 January 1890) the appeal had raised in excess of seven thousand pounds. The list of donors included the Jewish Rothschild family. Fr Pamphile de Veuster, Damien's brother, was guest of honour at the dinner and must have been wondering if it was all really happening.

Fr Damien's life and work have become widely known, and both he and Stevenson have been honoured and commemorated with statues and plaques. But the greatest monument to them both – and the one that tells us so much about each – remains the beautiful, powerful, somewhat reckless defence of Damien penned in Sydney by Robert Louis Stevenson.

Fr F.E. Burns

An Open Letter to the Reverend Dr. Hyde of Honolulu

SYDNEY,
FEBRUARY 25, 1890.

Sir, – It may probably occur to you that we have met, and visited, and conversed; on my side, with interest. You may remember that you have done me several courtesies, for which I was prepared to be grateful. But there are duties which come before gratitude, and offences which justly divide friends, far more acquaintances. Your letter to the Reverend H. B. Gage is a document which, in my sight, if you had filled me with bread when I was starving, if you had sat up to nurse my father when he lay a-dying, would yet absolve me from the bonds of gratitude. You know enough, doubtless, of the process of canonisation to be aware that, a hundred years after the death of Damien, there will appear a man charged with the painful office of the DEVIL'S ADVOCATE. After that noble brother of mine, and of all frail clay, shall have lain a century at rest, one shall accuse, one defend him. The circumstance is unusual that the devil's advocate should be a volunteer, should be a member of a sect immediately rival, and should make haste to take upon himself his ugly office ere the bones are cold; unusual, and of a taste which I shall leave my readers free to qualify; unusual, and to me inspiring. If I have at all learned the trade of using words to convey truth and to arouse emotion, you have at last furnished me with a subject. For it is in the interest of all mankind, and the cause of public decency in every quarter of the world, not only that Damien should be righted, but that you and your letter should be displayed at length, in their true colours, to the public eye.

To do this properly, I must begin by quoting you at large: I shall then proceed to criticise your utterance from several points of view, divine and human, in the course of which I shall attempt to draw again, and with more specification, the character of the dead saint whom it has pleased you to vilify: so much being done, I shall say farewell to you for ever.

"HONOLULU,
"AUGUST 2, 1889.
"Rev. H. B. GAGE.
"Dear Brother, – In answer to your inquires about Father Damien, I can only reply that we who knew the man are surprised at the extravagant newspaper laudations, as if he was a most saintly philanthropist. The simple truth is, he was a coarse, dirty man, headstrong and bigoted. He was not sent to Molokai, but went there without orders; did not stay at the leper settlement (before he became one himself), but circulated freely over the whole island (less than half the island is devoted to the lepers), and he came often to Honolulu. He had no hand in the reforms and improvements inaugurated, which were the work of our Board of Health, as occasion required and means were provided. He was not a pure man in his relations with women, and the leprosy of which he died should be

attributed to his vices and carelessness. Other have done much for the lepers, our own ministers, the government physicians, and so forth, but never with the Catholic idea of meriting eternal life. – Yours, etc.,
"C. M. HYDE"
[From the *Sydney Presbyterian*, 26 October 1889.]

To deal fitly with a letter so extraordinary, I must draw at the outset on my private knowledge of the signatory and his sect. It may offend others; scarcely you, who have been so busy to collect, so bold to publish, gossip on your rivals. And this is perhaps the moment when I may best explain to you the character of what you are to read: I conceive you as a man quite beyond and below the reticences of civility: with what measure you mete, with that shall it be measured you again; with you, at last, I rejoice to feel the button off the foil and to plunge home. And if in aught that I shall say I should offend others, your colleagues, whom I respect and remember with affection, I can but offer them my regret; I am not free, I am inspired by the consideration of interests far more large; and such pain as can be inflicted by anything from me must be indeed trifling when compared with the pain with which they read your letter. It is not the hangman, but the criminal, that brings dishonour on the house.

You belong, sir, to a sect – I believe my sect, and that in which my ancestors laboured – which has enjoyed, and partly failed to utilise, an exceptional advantage in the islands of Hawaii. The first missionaries came; they found the land already self-purged of its old and bloody faith; they were embraced, almost on their arrival, with enthusiasm; what troubles they supported came far more from whites than from Hawaiians; and to these last they stood (in a rough figure) in the shoes of God. This is not the place to enter into the degree or causes of their failure, such as it is. One element alone is pertinent, and must here be plainly dealt with. In the course of their evangelical calling, they – or too many of them – grew rich. It may be news to you that the houses of missionaries are a cause of mocking on the streets of Honolulu. It will at least be news to you, that when I returned your civil visit, the driver of my cab commented on the size, the taste, and the comfort of your home. It would have been news certainly to myself, had any one told me that afternoon that I should live to drag such a matter into print. But you see, sir, how you degrade better men to your own level; and it is needful that those who are to judge betwixt you and me, betwixt Damien and the devil's advocate, should understated your letter to have been penned in a house which could raise, and that very justly, the envy and the comments of the passers-by. I think (to employ a phrase of yours which I admire) it "should be attributed" to you that you have never visited the scene of Damien's life and death. If you had, and had recalled it, and looked about your pleasant rooms, even your pen perhaps would have been stayed.

Your sect (and remember, as far as any sect avows me, it is mine) has not done ill in a worldly sense in the Hawaiian Kingdom. When calamity befell their innocent parishioners, when leprosy descended and took root in the Eight Islands, a QUID PRO QUO was to be looked for. To that prosperous mission, and to you, as one of its adornments, God had sent at last an opportunity. I know I am touching here upon a nerve acutely sensitive. I know that others of your colleagues look back on the inertia of your Church, and the intrusive and decisive heroism of Damien, with something almost to be called remorse. I am sure it is so with yourself; I am persuaded your letter was inspired by a certain envy, not essentially ignoble, and the one human trait to be espied in that performance. You were thinking of the lost chance, the past day; of that which should have been conceived and was not; of the service due and not rendered. TIME WAS, said the voice in your ear, in your pleasant room, as you sat raging and writing; and if the words written were base beyond parallel, the rage, I am happy to repeat – it is the only compliment I shall pay you – the rage was almost virtuous. But, sir, when we have failed, and another has succeeded; when we have stood by, and another has stepped in; when we sit and grow bulky in our charming mansions, and a plain, uncouth peasant steps into the battle, under the eyes of God, and succours the afflicted, and consoles the dying, and is himself afflicted in his turn, and dies upon the field of honour – the battle cannot be retrieved as your unhappy irritation has suggested. It is a lost battle, and lost for ever. One thing remained to you in your defeat – some rags of common honour; and these you have made haste to cast away.

Common honour; not the honour of having done anything right, but the honour of not having done aught conspicuously foul; the honour of the inert: that was what remained to you. We are not all expected to be Damiens; a man may conceive his duty more narrowly, he may love his comforts better; and none will cast a stone at him for that. But will a gentleman of your reverend profession allow me an example from the fields of gallantry? When two gentlemen compete for the favour of a lady, and the one succeeds and the other is rejected, and (as will sometimes happen) matter damaging to the successful rival's credit reaches the ear of the defeated, it is held by plain men of no pretensions that his mouth is, in the circumstance, almost necessarily closed. Your Church and Damien's were in Hawaii upon a rivalry to do well: to help, to edify, to set divine examples. You having (in one huge instance) failed, and Damien succeeded, I marvel it should not have occurred to you that you were doomed to silence; that when you had been outstripped in that high rivalry, and sat inglorious in the midst of your well-being, in your pleasant room – and Damien, crowned with glories and horrors, toiled and rotted in that pigsty of his under the cliffs of Kalawao – you, the elect who would not, were the last man on earth to collect and propagate gossip on the volunteer who would and did.

I think I see you – for I try to see you in the flesh as I write these sentences – I think I see you leap at the word pigsty, a hyperbolical expression at the best. "He had no hand in the reforms," he was "a coarse, dirty man"; these were your own words; and you may think it possible that I am come to support you with fresh evidence. In a sense, it is even so. Damien has been too much depicted with a conventional halo and conventional features; so drawn by men who perhaps had not the eye to remark or the pen to express the individual; or who perhaps were only blinded and silenced by generous admiration, such as I partly envy for myself – such as you, if your soul were enlightened, would envy on your bended knees. It is the least defect of such a method of portraiture that it makes the path easy for the devil's advocate, and leaves the misuse of the slanderer a considerable field of truth. For the truth that is suppressed by friends is the readiest weapon of the enemy. The world, in your despite, may perhaps owe you something, if your letter be the means of substituting once for all a credible likeness for a wax abstraction. For, if that world at all remember you, on the day when Damien of Molokai shall be named a Saint, it will be in virtue of one work: your letter to the Reverend H. B. Gage.

You may ask on what authority I speak. It was my inclement destiny to become acquainted, not with Damien, but with Dr. Hyde. When I visited the lazaretto, Damien was already in his resting grave. But such information as I have, I gathered on the spot in conversation with those who knew him well and long: some indeed who revered his memory; but others who had sparred and wrangled with him, who beheld him with no halo, who perhaps regarded him with small respect, and through whose unprepared and scarcely partial communications the plain, human features of the man shone on me convincingly. These gave me what knowledge I possess; and I learnt it in that scene where it could be most completely and sensitively understood – Kalawao, which you have never visited, about which you have never so much as endeavoured to inform yourself; for, brief as your letter is, you have found the means to stumble into that confession. "LESS THAN ONE-HALF of the island," you say, "is devoted to the lepers." Molokai – "MOLOKAI AHINA," the "grey," lofty, and most desolate island – along all its northern side plunges a front of precipice into a sea of unusual profundity. This range of cliff is, from east to west, the true end and frontier of the island. Only in one spot there projects into the ocean a certain triangular and rugged down, grassy, stony, windy, and rising in the midst into a hill with a dead crater: the whole bearing to the cliff that overhangs it somewhat the same relation as a bracket to a wall. With this hint you will now be able to pick out the leper station on a map; you will be able to judge how much of Molokai is thus cut off between the surf and precipice, whether less than a half, or less than a quarter, or a fifth, or a tenth – or, say a twentieth; and the next time you burst into print you will be in a position to share with us the issue of your calculations.

I imagine you to be one of those persons who talk with cheerfulness of that place which oxen and wain-ropes could not drag you to behold. You, who do not even know its situation on the map, probably denounce sensational descriptions, stretching your limbs the while in your pleasant parlour on Beretania Street. When I was pulled ashore there one early morning, there sat with me in the boat two sisters, bidding farewell (in humble imitation of Damien) to the lights and joys of human life. One of these wept silently; I could not withhold myself from joining her. Had you been there, it is my belief that nature would have triumphed even in you; and as the boat drew but a little nearer, and you beheld the stairs crowded with abominable deformations of our common manhood, and saw yourself landing in the midst of such a population as only now and then surrounds us in the horror of a nightmare – what a haggard eye you would have rolled over your reluctant shoulder towards the house on Beretania Street! Had you gone on; had you found every fourth face a blot upon the landscape; had you visited the hospital and seen the butt-ends of human beings lying there almost unrecognisable, but still breathing, still thinking, still remembering; you would have understood that life in the lazaretto is an ordeal from which the nerves of a man's spirit shrink, even as his eye quails under the brightness of the sun; you would have felt it was (even today) a pitiful place to visit and a hell to dwell in. It is not the fear of possible infection. That seems a little thing when compared with the pain, the pity, and the disgust of the visitor's surroundings, and the atmosphere of affliction, disease, and physical disgrace in which he breathes. I do not think I am a man more than usually timid; but I never recall the days and nights I spent upon that island promontory (eight days and seven nights), without heartfelt thankfulness that I am somewhere else. I find in my diary that I speak of my stay as a "grinding experience": I have once jotted in the margin, "HARROWING is the word"; and when the *Mokolii* bore me at last towards the outer world, I kept repeating to myself, with a new conception of their pregnancy, those simple words of the song –

"'Tis the most distressful country that ever yet was seen."

And observe: that which I saw and suffered from was a settlement purged, bettered, beautified; the new village built, the hospital and the Bishop-Home excellently arranged; the sisters, the doctor, and the missionaries, all indefatigable in their noble tasks. It was a different place when Damien came there and made this great renunciation, and slept that first night under a tree amidst his rotting brethren: alone with pestilence; and looking forward (with what courage, with what pitiful sinkings of dread, God only knows) to a lifetime of dressing sores and stumps.

You will say, perhaps, I am too sensitive, that sights as painful abound in cancer hospitals and are confronted daily by doctors and nurses. I have long learned to admire and envy the doctors and the nurses. But there is no cancer hospital so large and populous as Kalawao and Kalaupapa; and in such a matter every fresh case, like every inch of length in the pipe of an organ, deepens the note of the impression; for what daunts the onlooker is that monstrous sum of human suffering by which he stands surrounded. Lastly, no doctor or nurse is called upon to enter once for all the doors of that gehenna; they do not say farewell, they need not abandon hope, on its sad threshold; they but go for a time to their high calling, and can look forward as they go to relief, to recreation, and to rest. But Damien shut-to with his own hand the doors of his own sepulchre.

I shall now extract three passages from my diary at Kalawao.

A. "Damien is dead and already somewhat ungratefully remembered in the field of his labours and sufferings. 'He was a good man, but very officious,' says one. Another tells me he had fallen (as other priests so easily do) into something of the ways and habits of thought of a Kanaka; but he had the wit to recognise the fact, and the good sense to laugh at it. A plain man it seems he was; I cannot find he was a popular."

B. "After Ragsdale's death" [Ragsdale was a famous Luna, or overseer, of the settlement] "there followed a brief term of office by Father Damien which served only to publish the weakness of that noble man. He was rough in his ways, and he had no control. Authority was relaxed; Damien's life was threatened, and he was soon eager to resign."

C. "Of Damien I begin to have an idea. He seems to have been a man of the peasant class, certainly of the peasant type: shrewd, ignorant and bigoted, yet with an open mind, and capable of receiving and digesting a reproof if it were bluntly administered; superbly generous in the least thing as well as in the greatest, and as ready to give his last shirt (although not without human grumbling) as he had been to sacrifice his life; essentially indiscreet and officious, which made him a troublesome colleague; domineering in all his ways, which made him incurably unpopular with the Kanakas, but yet destitute of real authority, so that his boys laughed at him and he must carry out his wishes by the means of bribes. He learned to have a mania for doctoring; and set up the Kanakas against the remedies of his regular rivals: perhaps (if anything matter at all in the treatment of such a disease) the worst thing that he did, and certainly the easiest. The best and worst of the man appear very plainly in his dealings with Mr. Chapman's money; he had originally laid it out entirely for the benefit of Catholics, and even so not wisely; but after a long, plain talk, he admitted his error fully and revised the list. The sad state of the boys' home is in part the result of his lack of control; in part, of his own slovenly ways and false ideas of hygiene. Brother officials used to call it 'Damien's Chinatown.' 'Well,' they would say, 'your Chinatown keeps growing.' And he would laugh with perfect good-nature, and adhere to his errors with perfect obstinacy. So much I have gathered of truth about this plain, noble human brother and father of ours; his imperfections are the traits of his face, by which we know him for our fellow; his martyrdom and his example nothing can lessen or annul; and only a person here on the spot can properly appreciate their greatness."

I have set down these private passages, as you perceive, without correction; thanks to you, the public has them in their bluntness. They are almost a list of the man's faults, for it is rather these that I was seeking: with his virtues, with the heroic profile of his life, I and the world were already sufficiently acquainted. I was besides a little suspicious of Catholic testimony; in no ill sense, but merely because Damien's admirers and disciples were the least likely to be critical. I know you will be more suspicious still; and the facts set down above were one and all collected from the lips of Protestants who had opposed the father in his life. Yet I am strangely deceived, or they build up the image of a man, with all his weakness, essentially heroic, and alive with rugged honesty, generosity, and mirth.

Take it for what it is, rough private jottings of the worst sides of Damien's character, collected from the lips of those who had laboured with and (in your own phrase) "knew the man"; – though I question whether Damien would have said that he knew you. Take it, and observe with wonder how well you were served by your gossips, how ill by your intelligence and sympathy; in how many points of fact we are at one, and how widely our appreciations vary. There is something wrong here; either with you or me. It is possible, for instance, that you, who seem to have so many ears in Kalawao, had heard of the affair of Mr. Chapman's money, and were singly struck by Damien's intended wrong-doing. I was struck with that also, and set it fairly down; but I was struck much more by the fact that he had the honesty of mind to be convinced.

I may here tell you that it was a long business; that one of his colleagues sat with him late into the night, multiplying arguments and accusations; that the father listened as usual with "perfect good-nature and perfect obstinacy"; but at the last, when he was persuaded – "Yes," said he, "I am very much obliged to you; you have done me a service; it would have been a theft." There are many (not Catholics merely) who require their heroes and saints to be infallible; to these the story will be painful; not to the true lovers, patrons, and servants of mankind.

And I take it, this is a type of our division; that you are one of those who have an eye for faults and failures; that you take a pleasure to find and publish them; and that, having found them, you make haste to forget the overvailing virtues and the real success which had alone introduced them to your knowledge. It is a dangerous frame of mind. That you may understand how dangerous, and into what a situation it has already brought you, we will (if you please) go hand-in-hand through the different phrases of your letter, and candidly examine each from the point of view of its truth, its appositeness, and its charity.

Damien was COARSE.

It is very possible. You make us sorry for the lepers, who had only a coarse old peasant for their friend and father. But you, who were so refined, why were you not there, to cheer them with the lights of culture? Or may I remind you that we have some reason to doubt if John the Baptist were genteel; and in the case of Peter, on whose career you doubtless dwell approvingly in the pulpit, no doubt at all he was a "coarse, headstrong" fisherman! Yet even in our Protestant Bibles Peter is called Saint.

Damien was DIRTY.

He was. Think of the poor lepers annoyed with this dirty comrade! But the clean Dr. Hyde was at his food in a fine house.

Damien was HEADSTRONG.

I believe you are right again; and I thank God for his strong head and heart.

Damien was BIGOTED.

I am not fond of bigots myself, because they are not fond of me. But what is meant by bigotry, that we should regard it as a blemish in a priest? Damien believed his own religion with the simplicity of a peasant or a child; as I would I could suppose that you do. For this, I wonder at him some way off; and had that been his only character, should have avoided him in life. But the point of interest in Damien, which has caused him to be so much talked about and made him at last the subject of your pen and mine, was that, in him, his bigotry, his intense and narrow faith, wrought potently for good, and strengthened him to be one of the world's heroes and exemplars.

Damien WAS NOT SENT TO MOLOKAI, BUT WENT THERE WITHOUT ORDERS.
Is this a misreading? or do you really mean the words for blame? I have heard Christ, in the pulpits of our Church, held up for imitation on the ground that His sacrifice was voluntary. Does Dr. Hyde think otherwise?

Damien DID NOT STAY AT THE SETTLEMENT, ETC.
It is true he was allowed many indulgences. Am I to understand that you blame the father for profiting by these, or the officers for granting them? In either case, it

is a mighty Spartan standard to issue from the house on Beretania Street; and I am convinced you will find yourself with few supporters.

Damien HAD NO HAND IN THE REFORMS, ETC.
I think even you will admit that I have already been frank in my description of the man I am defending; but before I take you up upon this head, I will be franker still, and tell you that perhaps nowhere in the world can a man taste a more pleasurable sense of contrast than when he passes from Damien's "Chinatown" at Kalawao to the beautiful Bishop-Home at Kalaupapa. At this point, in my desire to make all fair for you, I will break my rule and adduce Catholic testimony. Here is a passage from my diary about my visit to the Chinatown, from which you will see how it is (even now) regarded by its own officials: "We went round all the dormitories, refectories, etc. – dark and dingy enough, with a superficial cleanliness, which he" [Joseph Dutton, a lay brother] "did not seek to defend. 'It is almost decent,' said he; 'the sisters will make that all right when we get them here.'" And yet I gathered it was already better since Damien was dead, and far better than when he was there alone and had his

own (not always excellent) way. I have now come far enough to meet you on a common ground of fact; and I tell you that, to a mind not prejudiced by jealousy, all the reforms of the lazaretto, and even those which he most vigorously opposed, are properly the work of Damien. They are the evidence of his success; they are what his heroism provoked from the reluctant and the careless. Many were before him in the field; Mr. Meyer, for instance, of whose faithful work we hear too little: there have been many since; and some had more worldly wisdom, though none had more devotion, than our saint. Before his day, even you will confess, they had effected little. It was his part, by one striking act of martyrdom, to direct all men's eyes on that distressful country. At a blow, and with the price of his life, he made the place illustrious and public. And that, if you will consider largely, was the one reform needful; pregnant of all that should succeed. It brought money; it brought (best individual addition of them all) the sisters; it brought supervision, for public opinion and public interest landed with the man at Kalawao. If ever any man brought reforms, and died to bring them, it was he. There is not a clean cup or towel in the Bishop-Home, but dirty Damien washed it.

Damien WAS NOT A PURE MAN IN HIS RELATIONS WITH WOMEN, ETC.

How do you know that? Is this the nature of conversation in that house on Beretania Street which the cabman envied, driving past? – racy details of the misconduct of the poor peasant priest, toiling under the cliffs of Molokai?

Many have visited the station before me; they seem not to have heard the rumour. When I was there I heard many shocking tales, for my informants were men speaking with the plainness of the laity; and I heard plenty of complaints of Damien. Why was this never mentioned? and how came it to you in the retirement of your clerical parlour?

But I must not even seem to deceive you. This scandal, when I read it in your letter, was not new to me. I had heard it once before; and I must tell you how. There came to Samoa a man from Honolulu; he, in a public-house on the beach, volunteered the statement that Damien had "contracted the disease from having connection with the female lepers"; and I find a joy in telling you how the report was welcomed in a public-house. A man sprang to his feet; I am not at liberty to give his name, but from what I heard I doubt if you would care to have him to dinner in Beretania Street. "You miserable little -------" (here is a word I dare not print, it would so shock your ears). "You miserable little ------," he cried, "if the story were a thousand times true, can't you see you are a million times a lower ----- for daring to repeat it?" I wish it could be told of you that when the report reached you in your house, perhaps after family worship, you had found in your soul enough holy anger to receive it with the same expressions; ay, even with that one which I dare not print; it would not need to have been blotted away, like Uncle Toby's oath, by the tears of the recording angel; it would have been counted to you for your brightest righteousness. But you have deliberately chosen the part of the man from Honolulu, and you have played it with improvements of your own. The man from Honolulu – miserable, leering creature – communicated the tale to a rude knot of beach-combing drinkers in a public-house, where (I will so far agree with your temperance opinions) man is not always at his noblest; and the man from Honolulu had himself been drinking – drinking, we may charitably fancy, to excess. It was to your "Dear Brother, the Reverend H. B. Gage," that you chose to communicate the sickening story; and the blue ribbon which adorns your portly bosom forbids me to allow you the extenuating plea that you were drunk when it was done. Your "dear brother" – a brother indeed – made haste to deliver up your letter (as a means of grace, perhaps) to the religious papers; where, after many months, I found and read and wondered at it; and whence I have now reproduced it for the wonder of others. And you and your dear brother have, by this cycle of operations, built up a contrast very edifying to examine in detail. The man whom you would not care to have to dinner, on the one side; on the other, the Reverend Dr. Hyde and the Reverend H. B. Gage: the Apia bar-room, the Honolulu manse.

But I fear you scarce appreciate how you appear to your fellow-men; and to bring it home to you, I will suppose your story to be true. I will suppose – and God forgive me for supposing it – that Damien faltered and stumbled in his narrow path of duty; I will suppose that, in the horror of his isolation, perhaps in the fever of incipient disease, he, who was doing so much more than he had sworn, failed in the letter of his priestly oath – he, who was so much a better man than either you or me, who did what we have never dreamed of daring – he too tasted of our common frailty. "O, Iago, the pity of it!" The least tender should be moved to tears; the most incredulous to prayer. And all that you could do was to pen your letter to the Reverend H. B. Gage!

Is it growing at all clear to you what a picture you have drawn of your own heart? I will try yet once again to make it clearer. You had a father: suppose this tale were about him, and some informant brought it to you, proof in hand: I am not making too high an estimate of your emotional nature when I suppose you would regret the circumstance? that you would feel the tale of frailty the more keenly since it shamed the author of your days? and that the last thing you would do would be to publish it in the religious press? Well, the man who tried to do what Damien did, is my father, and the father of the man in the Apia bar, and the father of all who love goodness; and he was your father too, if God had given you grace to see it.

Robert Louis Stevenson

AFTERWORD
The Grace to See It

Presbyterianism has never attempted to take its place in this world through the gentle art of subtlety. Indeed the Presbyterian magician may find himself equally applauded for extracting rabbits from a hat by employing the services of a pitchfork as by the use of a more discreet and genteel method. I write this from the perspective of a Presbyterian cleric of some twenty years.

Robert Louis Stevenson was a Presbyterian raised on a diet of Scottish oats and hell. Speaking of his childhood he once said, 'I would lie awake to weep for Jesus, but I would fear to trust myself to slumber lest I was not accepted and would slip, ere I awoke, into eternal ruin.' The church has always preached hell better than heaven because fear makes for better tyranny than comfort. So as Stevenson grew up, hell was a bloated companion whose presence could be assumed whereas 'grace and comfort' were emaciated twins who rarely if ever showed up.

Presbyterianism still carries the shadow of this harsh and sober thinking and must search within to find answers as to how to present itself to the modern mind. If after some time a formula seems flawed, the best response is not to change the laboratory and perform the same formula with even more gusto. Sometimes one has to change the formula, the principle or the modus operandi rather than simply reach for a megaphone to broadcast more forcibly what we have already learned is not working.

Our world is a changing place, the old and well-known expressions of faith seem to be waning, and yet people's appetite for spiritual matters seems to be on the rise. I do not believe churches need to reinvent themselves or search for some elusive and long lost elixir. We simply need to find the core expression of human affection, the everlasting formula that has transformed countless thousands of people through all the thousands of countless years that we have been recording the notable actions of people.

When we find one such act, one such note of human impression, we always record the place and time within our minds as a wonderful grassy pasture where the best of human action fell from heaven as manna. But those stories we fear belong to the world of fairy tales. Cinderellas are rarely found in hotel suites and today's Sleeping Beauties are usually surrounded by plain working dwarves rather than handsome princes. You may hope that Prince Charming will rescue you from your imprisoning tower but you know it is more likely to be a man in a white transit van than a knight on a dashing white steed!

To speed us on our journey, to assist our quest to the centre of all things noble, we can find no better companion than Robert Louis Stevenson taking us to the island of Molokai. You won't find this trip advertised in the window of a travel agent, for it involves the dissolution of all things learned and the dereliction of all denominationalism anchored in pride.

The island of Molokai is the 'parenthesis of all prejudices' where a hellish smoke of fear, ignorance and bigotry rose up from what was otherwise a little slice of geographical heaven. But now that smoke has cleared, we find in the ashes of three lives – the lives of Stevenson, Fr Damien and Rev. Dr Hyde – answers to our deepest questions about the essence of all things noble.

When Stevenson arrived on Molokai, he discovered in the truest sense that hell does have coordinates:

> As the boat drew nearer [we] beheld the stairs crowded with abominable deformations of our common manhood ... a population as only now and then surrounds us in the horror of a nightmare ... the butt-ends of human beings lying there almost unrecognisable but still breathing, still thinking, still remembering ... a pitiful place to visit, a hell to dwell in.

He also discovered that the formula with the greatest capacity to transform people lies not in the beauty of the petal but in the ugliness of the root. Neither a petal nor a fairy tale beauty, Damien was the root of all good things that came to pass upon the island. The formula of transforming goodness was not in the sweet aroma of human perfection but rather in the brutal ugliness of human sacrifice.

It was his part, by one striking act of martyrdom, to direct all men's eyes on that distressful country. At a blow, and with the price of his life, he made the place illustrious and public. And that, if you will consider largely, was the one reform needful; pregnant of all that should succeed. It brought money; it brought (best individual addition of them all) the sisters; it brought supervision, for public opinion and public interest landed with the man at Kalawao.

What roused Stevenson to so defend the priest called Fr Damien, a man the great author never tries to present as an example of pure virtue or human perfection? What inspired him among the ashes of human deformation that he encountered on the island? I believe he felt that Damien's sacrifice was a notable act of human mercy and that Damien had been wronged by the unfavourable pen of Hyde. But rising above that like the cliffs of Kalawao was another less-articulated motivation that drove Stevenson's unfettered sail of words.

The scene of 'abominable deformations of our common manhood' took the writer to a theological island, which, once envisioned, pushed him forward to craft his letter to

Hyde, as though compelled and completely careless as to what others, or what any Presbyterian fellows, would think about him. It is my opinion that Stevenson saw in Damien a picture or shadow of Christ. Not so much in the personal virtues of the man, for these he admits were not those of Christ, but simply a shadow. A shadow is not the reality, it is not the fullness, nor even the person, but simply a herald, an impression or a provocation to ponder the reality. It is a one-dimensional and greyscale interpretation of a rainbow of divine proportions. And while Stevenson never pretends that Damien wore a halo like a character who has stepped out of a celestial artwork, he did see a light around him that demonstrated something of what is most significant in life.

When Stevenson looked upon the brutal scene of Molokai, the place Damien inhabited, he saw in his mind's eye a fleeting shadow of Christ on a theological island which represented the world. The terrain of a writer is imagination and once conjured there is no containing or returning it to its place of origin. The more Stevenson saw, the more he saw Christ in the leper priest. In the actions of Damien he saw a shadow of Christ coming from a better world, a better place called heaven. He saw him come down the cliff of descent to a world of suffering. He saw in Damien's voluntary journey to the leper colony, Christ's voluntary arrival in this world.

Stevenson had his own faith struggles, yet his childhood learning reminded him that all were sinners and the suggestion that one person's sin is less than another's is like a swimmer drowning in a sea of manure convincing himself that his position is enviable compared to a man drowning in an ocean of the stuff. He recalled the passages of the Bible that speak of Christ living and tenting among us, we who are diseased and ridden with sin like blemished and loathsome sores. That was his Presbyterian mind, that was what he had learned in his catechisms. Indeed it is this belief that brings us to another destination. Not only does Jesus come to this world, but he takes upon himself our disease of sin and on a cross outside the city of Jerusalem he died, despised and rejected.

Of course it would not have passed by Stevenson's attention that Jesus when approached once by a leper reached out and touched him. He healed him too, but only after he had touched him. If we were advisers to the divine we might suggest he reverse the order: heal first and touch later, but Jesus wanted the leper to know he was loved and accepted in the state of his disease.

With noble language Stevenson wrote to Hyde, 'The man who did what Damien did is my father ... and the father of all who love goodness: and he was your father too, if God had given you the grace to see it.' Punctuated throughout his letter is this one singular and recurring theme, the ability to see, by grace, not just Damien's sacrifice but how it resembled the sacrifice of Christ. Stevenson had seen it and he shaped words to express what he had seen with an urgency, as though he were a man in a darkened room surrounded by others all wearing shades.

Realising that Hyde, writing from his fine mansion, saw none of this vista, Stevenson felt compelled to write with an apostolic gravitas, pursuing his task as relentlessly as an undertaker at a graveside. His letter to Hyde is pregnant with biblical imagery but none more so than this line referring to Damien: 'A plain, uncouth peasant steps into the battle, under the eyes of God.' Stevenson clearly wishes to put us in mind of David and Goliath. More importantly he is reminding us that every age has its Goliaths to be defeated and every age will offer Davids equal to the task.

Prejudice and bigotry, narrow religion and jealousies still stalk our landscapes like malignant giants. The spirit of Fr Damien is the spirit of all who step forward into the battle. These people may come from the least expected quarters. They are not plastic saviours with neon halos but people from the scarred and concrete streets of real life, and when we meet them we know that we have been in the presence of something special.

Rev. Keith Drury

Artist's Statement

Art is no more than a collection of pigments arranged as the artist finds useful to convey his intentions. Art at the lower end simply conveys feelings, a girl on a beach or a tranquil river. But to me, art at the higher end must aspire to do more. The best art has always informed and challenged. Some of the greatest shapers of our societies in the past have been artists who spoke out through their medium. Artobiography is the style I have developed to do precisely that, a form of mixed media where documents and words are layered on to a canvas and then sealed before over-painting with oils.

When asked to create a piece for the cover of this book, I immediately decided that it should not be painted with soft hues and gentle strokes, for there is nothing soft about leprosy, Molokai or the life Fr Damien lived. I also chose to paint the older, weathered Damien rather than the softer images of him as a young man. Damien had hard edges, as the letter penned by Robert Louis Stevenson indicates, and as an artist I have not tried to romanticise him but rather to present him as the raw hero and Saint he was.

The words behind the face seek to articulate the larger story. Sections of Stevenson's letter are included, along with pieces about Damien, about Molokai and about leprosy. This painting speaks of bigotry, hate and ignorance, but its message is about de-stigmatising leprosy. I am encouraged that this book will help bring relief to those suffering from AIDS in South Africa through the Desmond Tutu HIV Foundation. Too often HIV/AIDS sufferers experience the very same bigotry, hatred, ignorance and ostracisation that Damien and the lepers of Molokai experienced. Let us de-stigmatise AIDS now.

A variety of conventional and artobiographical art pieces may be viewed on the artist's website: www.artobiography.co.uk.

Rev. Keith Drury

Further Reading

J.H. Brocker, *Father Damien: The Lands of Kalaupapa* (1998); M. Bunson, *Father Damien: The Man and His Era* (1997); H.E. Crouch, *Two Josephs on Molokai: Damien and Dutton* (1998); G. Daws, *Holy Man: Father Damien of Molokai* (1984); H. Eynikel, *Molokai: The Story of Father Damien* (1999); J. Farrow, *Damien the Leper* (1998); G. MacNiven-Johnston, *Father Damien* (2009); Fr Pamphile (ed.), *Life and Letters of Fr Damien* (1899); A. and E. Sheehan, *Father Damien and the Bells* (2004); R. Stewart, *Leper Priest of Molokai: Father Damien* (2000).

Websites
Comprehensive website on Fr Damien:
www.leperpriest.blogspot.com
Congregation of the Sacred Hearts of Jesus and Mary:
www.ssccpicpus.com
Congregation of the Sacred Hearts of Jesus and Mary,
Ireland: www.sacredhearts.ie

Acknowledgements

I wish to thank the many friends and associates who helped in the creation of this book.

I must first thank Steven Reynaert, who, when I visited Flanders in August 2008, asked if I knew of Fr Damien, thereby releasing a flood of fond memories of a childhood hero. It was Steven who first informed me that Fr Damien was soon to be canonised. I must also thank Steven's Belgian colleagues: Patrick Florisson, Caroline Decoster, Philippe Delmotte and Franka Ferla.

Very special thanks are owed to everyone who contributed to this publication: Fr F.E. Burns, Rev. Keith Drury, Lavinia Crawford-Browne of the Desmond Tutu HIV Foundation and, posthumously, Robert Louis Stevenson and Rev. Hyde.

Thank you also to Seamus Cashman, my forever encouraging publishing mentor; editor Jennifer Armstrong and designer Glen Powell.

Special thanks are offered to the Sisters of Mercy; to Fr Aidan Carroll and Todd Allen, two good friends for many years; and to the late Gabriel Burke, godfather to my wife, Margaret.

Thank you to Fr Eamon Aylward, SS.CC., an Irish member of Fr Damien's order who has, for the past year, been a source of support and encouragement; to the Irish and international websites of the Congregation of the Sacred Hearts of Jesus and Mary for permission to use photographs of Fr Damien, Sr Marianne and Molokai; and to Bishop Patrick K. Lynch, SS.CC., for permission to quote from his work. Thanks also to Hugh E. Gentry and the Associated Press; the Grill Collection of the National Arts Club; Fr Martin Smith of *Africa Magazine*; and Fathers Pat and Brian Corcoran for the use of their photographs.

Finally, thanks are due to my ever-faithful, patient and sustaining family: Margaret, Therese, Carl, Emma, Moya, Liam, Cathal and Deirdre, their families, friends and associates. And to my late parents, Charles and Sara Mullan, who first inspired me with stories about Fr Damien.

Don Mullan

Desmond Tutu HIV Foundation

Desmond Tutu has exemplified the life of faith and service to which we as Christians are called. He has given his name to the Desmond Tutu HIV Foundation out of his deep concern for the immense burden the HI virus has placed on the well-being of South African citizens, especially the poor and those least able to fend for themselves, our children.

The Foundation is an 'action-research' organisation which aims to address the challenges created by this pandemic through community-based prevention, treatment and training. Many of the staff come from the communities in which they work. Pairing community-driven development and internationally acclaimed research, the DTHF envisions a brighter future where HIV is manageable and its presence diminished.

Help us, with Desmond Tutu, to realise this goal.

Enquiries:
Desmond Tutu HIV Foundation
P O Box 13901
Mowbray 7705
Cape Town
Tel: 0027 21 633 6599
lavinia.browne@hiv-research.org.za
www.desmondtutuhivcentre.org.za

Donations may be made to:
Desmond Tutu HIV Foundation
Standard Bank
Branch code 024909
SWIFT STZAZAJJ
Account 071292861

FR F.E. BURNS is a retired priest of the Melbourne Archdiocese. He served as curate in the parishes of Wattle Park, Ashburton and Mornington before serving as Parish Priest for six years at Holy Spirit Manifold Heights, Geelong. He served 12 years as chaplain at St Bede's College, Mentone, during which he wrote a Masters thesis on *Catholic Boarding Schools For Boys In Victoria 1878-1985*. Fr Burns served as chaplain with the Royal Australian Air Force for 18 years. He has written several articles for Catholic publications in Melbourne.

REV. KEITH DRURY spent the majority of his working life as a Minister of Religion before taking the ultimate 'step of faith' to leave ministry in August 2009 to pursue art as a professional career. Although Keith has been serving with the Presbyterian Church in Ireland for some twenty years he has been painting and drawing for as long as he can remember. Keith first qualified from The Queen's University of Belfast with a degree in Business Administration and worked for a few years in Short Brothers Aircraft Factory before entering the Presbyterian Church Ministry and reading theology, again at Queen's University. After serving in a variety of parishes Keith's final post with the Presbyterian Church in Ireland focused on the commercial and corporate sectors of Belfast City Centre. On account of Keith's exposure to the broadest spectrums of society, both rural and urban, much of Keith's art has become motivated by telling the stories of people's lives and exploring Irish socio-cultural dilemmas. His art is finished in oils on mixed media and has become known as 'artobiographical' creating a niche demand for both personal and corporate commissions. Convinced that the true essence of our Irish identity is story telling, Keith seeks to use art to help make people's lives and their culture accessible to others through the medium of oils.

Keith's art can also be viewed through a number of commercial galleries in the more traditional format of oils portraying cityscapes of Ireland.

DON MULLAN is the author of the acclaimed bestsellers, *Eyewitness Bloody Sunday* (Wolfhound Press, 1997) and *The Dublin and Monaghan Bombings* (Wolfhound Press, 2000). He has edited and authored several other books including his boyhood memoir, *Gordon Banks: A Hero Who Could Fly* (a little book company, 2006). Mullan was co-producer and associate producer on a trilogy of award-winning movies that explored the beginning, end and aftermath of the Northern Ireland conflict: *Bloody Sunday* (2002); *Omagh* (2004) and *Five Minutes of Heaven* (2009). He is currently working on projects exploring the themes of Sport for Development and Peace, including *The Christmas Truce Project* and *The Flanders Peace Field*, inspired by the remarkable and spontaneous truce that brought peace to the trenches on Christmas Day 1914. In March 2009, Mullan was welcomed by the Brazilian football legend, Pelé, as the first European Ambassador to represent the Pelé Little Prince Hospital, Curitiba, Brazil. He is also developing a series of Desmond and Leah Tutu Peace Choirs throughout the world. He is married with three children and lives in Dublin, Ireland.